WHAT GLORIOUS TIMES THEY HAD ~ NELLIE McCLUNG

a satire
by Diane Grant and Company

We would like to express our gratitude to The Canada Council and the Ontario Arts Council for their support.

Marian M. Wilson, Publisher

WHAT GLORIOUS TIMES THEY HAD — NELLIE McCLUNG
© Copyright 1974 by Diane Grant & Company
All rights reserved

No part of this book may be reproduced or transmitted in any form by any means, electronic or mechanical, including photocopying and recording, information storage and retrieval systems, without permission in writing from the publisher, except by a reviewer who may quote brief passages in a review.

Professionals and amateurs are hereby warned that this play is subject to royalty, being fully protected under the copyright laws of the Dominion of Canada and the United States of America, and all countries covered by the International Copyright Union, and all countries covered by the Pan-American Copyright Convention, and the Universal Copyright Convention.

All rights, including professional, amateur, motion picture, recitation, lecturing, public reading, radio broadcasting, television, and the rights of translation into foreign languages, are strictly reserved. Particular emphasis is laid on the question of readings, permission for which must be secured in writing. **All inquiries should be addressed to the authors** c/o Simon & Pierre Publishing Company Limited, P.O.Box 280 Adelaide Street Postal Station, Toronto, Ontario, Canada M5C 2J4.

Whenever the play is produced, the following notice must appear on all programs, printing and advertising for the play: "Produced by special arrangement with Simon & Pierre Publishing Company Limited". Authorship credit must be given on all programs, printing and advertising for the play.

ISBN 0-88924-048-5
1 2 3 4 5/79 78 77 76
Simon & Pierre Publishing Company Limited, Order Department
P.O.Box 280 Adelaide Street Postal Station
Toronto, Ontario, Canada M5C 2J4

Author  **Diane Grant** began playwriting at the University of British Columbia in 1961 with a one-act play called FAZAR. She learned stagecraft as an apprentice with Toronto Workshop Productions and has since worked as an actress and director in various theatres throughout Canada. Her last engagement was with the Stratford Festival as Melinda Moorhill in Brecht's TRUMPETS AND DRUMS.

She became interested in playwriting again while directing a documentary about the Toronto Islanders, called I'M HANLAN, I'M DURNAN, HE'S WARD. After completing work on WHAT GLORIOUS TIMES THEY HAD, she again collaborated with Redlight Theatre on a play about the comic strip character, Broom Hilda. She has just finished co-writing a Canadian film script with K.L.B. Feltham called A MILD SENSE OF DISAPPOINTMENT.

Play background

How the play was developed

WHAT GLORIOUS TIMES THEY HAD began as an idea for a play about the life of Nellie McClung. Diane Grant began research by reading Nellie McClung's novels — thirteen in all — and by acquiring newspaper reports of her activities.

Diane wrote a scenario of chronological events and worked with the cast, scene by scene, improvising and writing. The cast members conducted their own research into their characters and provided new material and ideas.

The play has since been revised and reworked several times.

Credits Production photographs are by Anne Wordsworth.
Photograph of Political Equality League, page E6, appears with special thanks to the Manitoba Archives, Winnipeg, Manitoba.

Original cast The play WHAT GLORIOUS TIMES THEY HAD was first produced by Redlight Theatre at Bathurst Street United Church, 736 Bathurst Street, Toronto, Ontario on May 8th, 1974 with the following cast:
Directed by Diane Grant
Musical Accompaniment by Monika Piebrock
Settings by Barbara Barron
Costumes by Heidi Grosowski
Photographs by Anne Wordsworth
Nellie McClung — Diane Grant
E. Cora Hind — Francine Volker
Frances Beynon — Jacquie Presly
Lillian Beynon Thomas — Elizabeth Murphy
Sir Rodmond Roblin — Geoffrey Saville-Read
P.T. Fletcher — Paul Brown

Original production notes

Casting

In the original production, actors doubled roles. E. Cora Hind doubled as a factory woman, Adelaide, and Evelyn. Lillian doubled as a factory woman and as Millicent.

One actor played Sir Rodmond Roblin and all other male roles were taken by the second actor.

An actor's change from one character to another was accomplished by a Brechtian technique using a change of hat, vest or veil. No attempt was made to disguise the actor, and sometimes the transformation was made onstage. However, there is no reason why a different actor cannot be used for each role.

The members of the Legislative Assembly and the Mock Parliament were represented by balloons which were used to suggest a large number of anonymous and obedient government backbenchers. This effect could also be achieved by using several actors dressed alike.

Staging
Although the play works equally well on a thrust stage or in the round, the first production was blocked for the proscenium. Minimal hand props, seven chairs and three moveable desks denoted different objects and places.

Lighting
The stage was divided into six lighting areas and actors changed

scenes by moving themselves and the furniture from one area to another.

A follow spot is suggested for several of the scenes.

There is a diagram of lighting areas on page E79.

Music
In the original production, one violin provided musical accompaniment, but any other instrument or instrumental group is possible if it evokes the "ladies' musical social" atmosphere.

Cast of characters **Sir Rodmond Roblin,** the Premier of Manitoba; a portly, dignified man in his early sixties
P.T.Fletcher, the parliamentary secretary to Sir Rodmond Roblin
Nellie McClung, a social reformer, novelist and suffragist; an attractive woman in her thirties
Frances Beynon, a journalist and suffragist
Lillian Beynon Thomas, a journalist and suffragist, Frances' sister
E. Cora Hind, an agriculture expert and journalist; a forceful woman in her early fifties
Mr. Wilson, a rancher from Calgary, Alberta
Gerry, an insurance clerk
Mr. Black, the boss to Gerry
Adelaide Roblin, the wife to Sir Rodmond Roblin
Mr. Ackroyd, a factory owner
Two factory women, employees of Mr. Ackroyd's
C.P.Walker, a theatre magnate
A man, a petitioner for male suffrage
A charwoman
Evelyn, an eastern woman
Millicent, sister to Evelyn
Tobias Crawford Norris, leader of the Liberal Party; a man in his early fifties
Various members of the Legislative Assembly, male cast members
Various members of the Mock Parliament, female cast members

General setting The play is set in Winnipeg, Manitoba

Time Between 1912 and 1916

Act one *In area 1 there are three chairs facing front, set diagonally from right to left. In area 3 there are two chairs facing front, set diagonally from left to right. In area 6 there is one chair facing front.*

The actors and musician enter in black. The musician turns on the Tiffany lamp above her head. The lights in area 6 are turned up low. The musician tunes her violin. In the darkness, we hear the voices of Roblin and Fletcher.

Roblin: No woman, idiot, lunatic or criminal shall vote.

Fletcher: Elections Act, Dominion of Canada.

(A spot comes up on Nellie, facing front, centre stage.)

Scene **Nellie:** People still speak of womanhood as if it were a disease. They may be somewhat prejudiced. If prejudices belonged to the vegetable world, they would be described under the general heading of: Hardy Perennials — will grow in any soil, bloom without ceasing, require no cultivation; will do better if left alone. In regard to tenacity of life, no yellow old cat has anything on a prejudice. You may kill it with your own hands, bury it deep and sit on the grave and behold, the next day, it will walk in at the back door, purring. Take some of the prejudices regarding women that have been exploded and blown to pieces many, many times and yet walk among us today in the fullness of life and vigour. One of the oldest and falsest of our beliefs regarding women is that they are protected — that some way in the battle of life, they get the best of it. People talk of men's chivalry, that vague, indefinite quality which is supposed to transmute the common clay of life into gold. Chivalry is a magic word. It seems to breathe of foreign strands and moonlit groves and silver sands and knights and kings; it seems to tell of glorious deeds and waving plumes and prancing steeds and belted earls and things. People tell us of the good old days of chivalry when womanhood was really respected and reverenced, when brave knight rode forth to die for his lady love. But, in order to be really loved and respected, there was one hard and fast condition laid down, to which all women must conform. They must be beautiful — no getting out of that. They simply had to have starry eyes and golden hair, or pale, white and haughty brow and a laugh like a ripple of magic. Then they were alright and armoured knights would die for them quick as a wink. The homely women were all witches, dreadful witches, and they drowned them on public holidays, in the mill pond.

(Applause. Areas 1 and 2 come up as spot goes out. Lillian, Frances and Cora are seated, facing front — stage right. The women move down to area 2 which stays up as the musician plays the introduction to "Win Them, Win Them, One By One". Area 1 fades to black. They sing the song . . . .)

Women: Win new members day by day
We'll help win them, here's the way.
Just one way can this be done
We must win them, one by one.

So you win the one next to you
And I'll win the one next to me,
In all kinds of weather
We'll all work together
To see what can be done.

If you win the one next to you
And I win the one next to me,
In no time at all
We'll have them all
So win them, win them, one by one.

(In areas 3, 4, and 5, lights come up.)

Frances: Congratulations, Nellie.

Nellie: Thank you.

Cora: First class speech. I enjoyed it immensely.

(Cora exits upstage right.)

Nellie: Thank you, Cora.

Lillian: What's your next stop?

(Lillian moves one of stage right chairs to area 4.)

Nellie: Moosamin.

Frances: Will you be seeing Mrs. Burritt in Sturgeon River? She's asked for fifty petition forms.

(Frances moves one of stage right chairs to area 5. She exits upstage left.)

Nellie: Really.

Lillian: That's 1,500 signatures.

Nellie: I'll have to see if they'll fit in my suitcase.

(Nellie exits downstage right.)

Lillian: How many people are there in Sturgeon River, Cora?

Cora *(entering upstage right, with pamphlets)*: Eight hundred and seventy-five. Nellie, how old is Mrs. Burritt?

Nellie *(entering with suitcase, downstage right)*: Ninety-one.

Frances *(entering with petition forms, downstage left)*: Good night! *(Gives forms to Nellie)* I must make a note to order some more forms. We're running out of them already.

Lillian: That's wonderful.

(Lillian exits upstage right.)

Cora: Do include my Lucy Stone pamphlet, Nellie. I think it's rather good.

Nellie *(takes pamphlets)*: I wouldn't dream of leaving it out.

(Nellie puts petition forms and pamphlets in suitcase.)

Lillian *(entering with basket, downstage right)*: Here's a treat for the train.

Nellie: Oh, how nice, Lillian. Thank you. *(Takes basket from Lillian.)*

Lillian: Who are you staying with in Moosamin, Nellie?

Nellie: The MacMillans.

Cora: You lucky thing. Doesn't she set a generous table?

Nellie: She certainly does. Those lemon biscuits. Aren't they good, Cora?

Cora: "You need five cents worth of oil of lemon and five cents worth of citrate of ammonia. Otherwise, it's just a *(Cora and Nellie in unison)* plain beaten biscuit."

Nellie: I must run. I have to pick up my tickets.

Lillian: Oh, that reminds me. Did you get the tickets for "Ben Hur" tonight?

Frances: Yes, I did. *(To Cora)* Aunt Alice is coming, isn't she?

Lillian *(to Nellie)*: I'm sorry you'll miss it.

Nellie: Well, duty calls.

Cora: "And no one shall work for money and no one shall work for fame, but each for the joy of working . . . ." That's . . . .

Nellie: Kipling, you know.

(The women laugh. Nellie takes Cora's arm. A chorus of, "Goodbye", "Have a good trip", "Good luck". Frances and Lillian exit downstage right, and Fletcher enters upstage left, carrying a brown paper bag. He passes Nellie and Cora who are exiting upstage left.)

Fletcher *(without pleasure)*: Morning.

Nellie & Cora: Good morning.

Scene   **In The Park** *(Sir Rodmond Roblin enters from upstage right.)*

Fletcher: Good morning, Mr. Premier.

Roblin: Morning, Fletcher. Nice day.

Fletcher: Yes, sir.

(Roblin mimes taking seed from Fletcher's paper bag and begins to mime feeding pigeons.)

Roblin *(pointing to pigeon)*: I think old Ferguson is getting a little fat, don't you?

Fletcher: Yes, sir.

Roblin: Fletcher?

Fletcher *(brushing off pigeon)*: Shoo. Shoo. Yes, sir?

Roblin: There aren't many men who would cheat their wives out of their share of the property, are there?

Fletcher: Course not, sir.

Roblin: My God, a man is forced to support his wife, isn't he? What more does she want?

Fletcher: Trouble at home, sir?

Roblin: Runny poached eggs.

Fletcher: What?

Roblin: Adelaide. She's taken to reading the Free Press . . . . She's been burning the toast as well. It's all this suffragist business. *(Pause. Roblin takes a pamphlet from his pocket)* She got this pamphlet in the mail from the Political Equality League. I confiscated it. *(Fletcher nods wisely)* You know, I really think she's on their side.

Fletcher: So is Norris, sir. He had the whole gaggle of them down to the Liberal convention last week.

Roblin: That damned opportunist. He'll do anything to win the next election.

Fletcher *(sardonically)*: He says he thinks they're right.

Roblin: Right? Of course, they're not right. The man's a bachelor. What does he know? "Wives submit yourselves unto your own husbands, as unto the Lord." That's damn well right. "For the husband is the head of the wife, even as Christ is the head of the Church." Paul to the Ephesians, Chapter 5, Verse 22.

Fletcher: Harmony . . . a house needs harmony.

E11

Roblin: "Unto the woman he said, 'I will greatly multiply thy sorrow and thy conception; in sorrow thou shalt bring forth children and thy desire shall be to thy husband, and he shall rule over thee'."

Fletcher: Amen. *(Pause. Roblin resumes feeding pigeons.)*

Roblin: Here, Fergie.

Fletcher: You know, their heads are smaller. Their brains are probably smaller, too. Do you think they're smart enough to vote?

(Nellie enters downstage right, carrying suitcase.)

Roblin *(lifts his hat)*: Good day to you, madam.

Nellie: Good day to you, sir. *(She continues walking, stops, and looks back)* Lovely day.

Roblin & Fletcher: Lovely day.

(Nellie exits upstage left. The men watch her leave.)

Roblin *(ruminatively)*: You know, Fletcher. I believe you're right. Their heads are smaller.

(Roblin and Fletcher exit upstage left. Music: "Victory Bells" is playing as Frances enters from downstage right, wheeling on a desk. On the desk are a typewriter and a telephone. She wheels it into area 1 — lights stay up. Areas 2, 3, 4, and 5 — lights fade. She sits and begins to type as Al enters from upstage left. Al is a snappy dresser, a fast talker and he is chewing on a toothpick. He is a salesman for Purity Flour. Frances continues typing as "Victory Bells" fades and Al approaches her.)

Scene   Frances

Al *(brightly)*: Good morning, is this the Grain Grower's Guide?

Frances: Yes, it is. May I help you?

Al: Who is the editor of the women's page?

Frances: Why, that would be Frances Marion Beynon.

(Al takes chair from area 4, places it next to Frances and sits.)

Al: Tell him I'm here.

Frances: I'm Frances Marion Beynon.

Al *(unfazed)*: How do you do? Well, I won't waste your time, Mrs. Beynon.

Frances: Miss.

Al: Yes. I'm here on behalf of Purity Flour. Now, have you seen our latest advertising poster? *(Unrolls a large poster featuring a girl with pies, breads and cakes)* There she is. Miss Purity. Isn't she a peach?

Frances: Well, actually, we use your advertising regularly, Mr. . . . .

Al *(moving in)*: You can call me Al. Yes, I know you do and that's why I'm here. Frankly, Miss Beynon, I find your column distressing. Too many articles on politics, prohibition, child welfare. Where are the recipes?

Frances: But we just published a lovely recipe for prune aspic.

Al: Prune aspic. Where are the cakes, the pies, the tortes? What would life be like without blueberry turnovers?

Frances: Infinitely impoverished.

Al: Miss Beynon — Frances — you have a wonderful sense of humour but no sense of proportion. Your column is encouraging women to leave the kitchen. They'll join clubs. They'll go to meetings. *(Intimately)* Do you have any idea of what goes on in those meetings?

Frances: As a matter of fact, I do. I'm a member of the Political Equality League.

Al: Oh. *(Pause)* What does go on in those meetings?

Frances: We like to discuss ideas of importance in the world, such as woman suffrage. Are you interested in women getting the vote?

Al: Oh, no. Oh, no. Think of the consequences, Miss Beynon. Women will go out into the world, that dangerous, dirty world.

Frances: But Al, charwomen have been cleaning up that dirty world for years . . . going abroad at 5:30 in the morning.

Al *(emphatically)*: Well, that's fine. They're used to it. What I'm talking about is commerce, science, politics, engineering.

Frances: Oh, you mean it's the clean professions women should stay away from.

Al *(angrily)*: No, I mean they should stay in the kitchen. That's their proper sphere.

Frances: Well then, you may be interested in this. I just received a report that Cornell University has just enrolled twelve men in domestic science. They seem to have a natural aptitude for it.

Al: Sissies.

Frances: Oh, I don't think so. It says here that one is a member of the Varsity baseball team and one is in the glee club.

Al: Ah hah.

Frances: The point is that labour is sexless.

Al *(infuriated)*: That's not the point. *(Regains composure)* And that's not the issue. The issue here is flour. Pastry that appeals.

Frances: Oh, I see. *(She stands up and wheels desk upstage to area 4. Crossfade to area 4)* Al, I don't think you quite understand the kind of thing I want to get into my column.

(Al picks up the chair on which Frances has been sitting and follows her with it.)

Al: I want you to think about this recipe for orange torte. *(He attempts to slide chair under Frances as she pauses behind desk, which she leaves in area 4)* This'll make your mouth water. *(Frances continues moving into area 2. Area 2 comes up as she moves into it. Al leaves chair behind desk and pursues Frances)* You take two cups of flour.

(Lillian enters from downstage left. She meets Frances and Al in area 2.)

Lillian: Hello.

Al: How do you do?

Frances: May I present Mr. . . . .

Al: You can call me Al.

Frances: Al. My sister, Lillian Thomas.

Al: Charmed, Miss Thomas.

Lillian: Mrs.

Al: Of course.

Frances *(to Lillian)*: Will you be at the lecture next week?

Lillian: Yes, I will. *(The phone rings in area 4)* I must run.

Frances: See you then. 'Bye. *(The phone rings again.)*

Lillian: Goodbye.

Al: As I was saying, the secret's in the flour . . . *(Al and Frances exit downstage left, Al hot on Frances' heels. The phone rings and Lillian picks it up . . . .)*

Scene **Lillian**

Lillian: Manitoba Free Press. Lillian Beynon Thomas. Yes. My mail is still on my desk. I haven't opened it yet. Mrs. McKenna, I'm a journalist, not a lawyer. Uh huh. The Political Equality League has a pamphlet out on the Legal Status of Women. I'd be happy to send you one. Uh huh. Mrs. Ruth McKenna, R.R. 3, Fort Rouge. Fine. I'll send it right away. 'Bye. *(She hangs up phone and sorts through the mail)* Mrs. McKenna, Mrs. McKenna. *(She opens the letters and reads)* "Dear Mrs. Thomas, I read your column on Court Protection for women and I'm wondering if I could get it. I have been married for seventeen years. Everything was fine until about five years ago. We lost quite a bit of money and my husband started drinking all the time. We have one girl at home. She's ten, and when he gets drunk, he beats her up, too. I don't care so much about myself anymore, but I'm worried about Janet. What do you think I should do? Mrs. Ruth McKenna." *(She picks up phone)* Operator, a Mrs. Ruth McKenna, Fort Rouge. *(Crossfade to area*

3 as Roblin enters from downstage left and sits on chair. He is reading the pamphlet which he confiscated from Adelaide. Lillian picks up pamphlet from desk — crossfade to area 4) Hello. Lillian Thomas here. I just read your letter, Mrs. McKenna. Yes, I think that you should apply for Court Protection right away. You are eligible, I'm quite sure. *(Finds section in pamphlet)* Here it is. The Married Woman's Protection Act. Section Two.

(Crossfade to area 3.)

Roblin: A married woman may apply to a county court judge for an order of protection in case of . . . assault . . . desertion . . . persistent cruelty . . . habitual drunkeness . . . or wilful neglect of children.

(Crossfade to area 4.)

Lillian: Section Three. A married woman who has committed an act of adultery cannot obtain an order of protection under this Act. Section Four . . . . I beg your pardon? Of course. Section Three . . . .

(Crossfade to area 3.)

Roblin: A married woman who has committed an act of adultery cannot obtain an order of protection under this Act. Hmm.

(Crossfade to area 4.)

Lillian: Mrs. McKenna? Are you still there? Mrs. McKenna? *(Pause. She hangs up the phone)* Hmm.

(Lillian wheels desk to area 5 as Roblin exits. Crossfade to area 5. E. Cora Hind enters from downstage right, galley proof in hand. She is in high dudgeon. She walks briskly into area 5.)

Scene Cora

Cora: Blast it, blast it, blast it! They've signed it E. C. Hind again. It's E. Cora Hind! This column is written by a woman and I want everyone to know it. *(Sees Lillian)* Lillian, what are you doing here?

Lillian *(agitated)*: Who do you know in Fort Rouge?

Cora *(busy with proof)*: Fort Rouge. There's Helen and Bertha Wood. You met them last summer. There's Reverend Braden . . . .

Lillian: Reverend Braden. He's the one. I'll ask him to call on her. *(She starts to exit.)*

Cora *(still busy with proof)*: Call on who?

Lillian *(over her shoulder)*: Mrs. McKenna.

(Lillian exits downstage left. The telephone rings as Frances enters from upstage left.)

Cora *(picks up phone)*: Agriculture. Miss Hind. Ask him to come right up. *(Hangs up phone)* Good morning, Frances.

Frances: Good night, your office is a shambles. Are you ready for the lecture this afternoon?

Cora *(shuffles through papers on her desk)*: I have my notes here somewhere . . . weekly market report for the cheese factories . . . weekly market report for the creameries . . . last year's wheat crop estimates . . . last year's . . . ! *(Looks up, delighted)* An invitation to the Stampede . . . !

(Mr. Wilson enters from downstage left. He is a rancher from Alberta.)

Mr. Wilson: I hope you're going to be there, Miss Hind. We're looking forward to seeing you down our way.

Cora: I've already laid out my riding boots and breeches. *(To Frances)* Frances, meet Mr. Wilson from Calgary. Mr. Wilson . . . Miss Beynon. *(They nod)* How's the ranch?

Mr. Wilson: Fine, Miss Hind. You know, though, I might'a got stuck with some questionable bulls.

Cora: What's the trouble?

Mr. Wilson *(scratches head)*: Well, I only had a conception rate of forty-eight percent on eleven bulls this year.

Frances: Cora, I think I'll . . . .

Cora: I hope you checked the semen quality.

Mr. Wilson: Oh, yah . . . seems pretty good.

Cora: Any cryptochordism?

Frances: Cora, I . . . .

Cora *(to Frances)*: That's when one or both of the testicles haven't descended into the scrotal sac.

Mr. Wilson: Nope. They've all dropped down. I mean, both dropped down on all of 'em. You see what I mean.

Cora: I don't know what the problem could be.

Mr. Wilson: Yah, it's ticklish. *(Turns to go)* Well, I won't keep you, Miss Hind. Just came in to chew the fat.

(Cora watches him go, smiling. Mr. Wilson exits downstage left. Pause.)

Cora: Lovely man.

Frances *(faintly)*: I think I need a cup of tea.

Cora *(briskly)*: Now, Frances, that's what's the matter with you women today. Forever nibbling on cinnamon toast and drinking tea. What you need to build you up is a nice juicy beefsteak.

(Frances exits downstage right. Cora wheels her desk off upstage right, as Gerry enters downstage right, wheeling in desk on which there is a sign saying "Neepawa Insurance Agency". He wheels it into area 3. Nellie enters from downstage right. Crossfade from area 5 to area 3. Gerry is a young man whose voice is still not firmly placed. He enjoys his work.)

Scene   The Insurance Policy

Nellie *(places suitcase on desk)*: Good afternoon, Gerry.

Gerry: Oh, hi, Mrs. McClung. How's things?

Nellie: Just fine, Gerry.

Gerry: What'll it be today?

Nellie: The usual.

Gerry: Ten days coverage for two dollars. Right? *(Takes pen and Accident Insurance Policy from drawer of desk)* There you go. Just sign on the bottom line.

Nellie *(takes pen and policy and signs)*: Thank you, Gerry. There you are.

Gerry *(putting pen away)*: Where are you off to today?

Nellie: Moosamin.

(Nellie begins to read the Accident Insurance Policy.)

Gerry: It's nice there this time of year.

Nellie *(reading)*: Yes. The lilacs are in bloom.

Gerry: Oh, that's nice. Say, how's Wes and the kids?

Nellie *(still reading)*: They're fine. Jack has a cold. Runs right through the family.

Gerry: Colds are awful. I hate to get them. *(Suddenly)* Did you say Moosamin? You'd better hurry. The train leaves in four minutes.

Nellie *(startled)*: Four minutes! Thank you. *(She picks up suitcase and begins to exit downstage right)* Have a good day, Gerry.

(Nellie walks away, continuing to read policy. She turns it over.)

Gerry: 'Bye, Mrs. McClung.

(Nellie stops suddenly and turns back.)

Nellie: Gerry!

Gerry *(surprised)*: Oh, hi, Mrs. McClung. Short trip.

Nellie: Gerry, I've been buying this Accident Insurance Policy for a year and a half and I just read it. I'm not covered. Have you read it?

Gerry: No, I don't read them. I just sell them.

Nellie *(shows him the back of the policy)*: Look at that.

Gerry *(peers closely at paper)*: Gee, that's written kind of small, isn't it? Would you like to speak to someone who knows something about it?

Nellie: Yes, I would, Gerry. Thank you.

(As Nellie waits, the lights dim and Gerry puts on a coat and glasses, transforming himself into Mr. Black. Mr. Black is an older man who has been in the insurance game for many years. The lights come up.)

Mr. Black: Sit down, sit down. Mrs. McClung?

Nellie: Yes.

Mr. Black: Mr. Black. Problem?

Nellie: I have only three minutes to catch my train, so I'll be brief.

Mr. Black: I'm a busy man myself.

Nellie *(firmly)*: I'd like to read this to you. "If the insured be a male, he will be paid the full principal sum for the loss of both hands or both feet or the sight of both eyes. . . . If the insured be a male, he will be paid the full principal sum for the loss of one hand or one foot or the sight of one eye. . . . If the insured be a male, etc. etc. . . . loss shall mean with regard to hands and feet, actual severance above or through the wrist . . . ."

Mr. Black *(sharply)*: I'm quite aware of what's in the policy, Mrs. McClung.

Nellie: Then you know what's on the back. In the black border.

Mr. Black: Yes.

Nellie: Females are insured against death only.

Mr. Black: Surely you know why, Mrs. McClung.

Nellie: No, I don't, Mr. Black.

Mr. Black: Women are too sensitive to be trusted. They are victims of pure nerves in an accident. I remember one case . . . an hysterical woman who claimed that she was in shock after a minor collision in Moos . . . Moos . . . Moos . . .

Nellie: Moosamin?

Mr. Black: Whatever. Do you know what she was, Mrs. McClung? *(Pause)* Pregnant. Yes, pregnant. No, no. There'd be no end of trouble. They'd imagine they were hurt and it'd be impossible to tell.

Nellie: But surely, Mr. Black, you could check to see if they imagined they'd lost a foot or had a hand cut off.

Mr. Black *(pause)*: Is there anything else I can do for you, Mrs. McClung?

Nellie: Yes, I'd like my two dollars back.

Mr. Black: Certainly. *(Takes form from drawer)* Just fill in this form and your money will be mailed to you in ten days in postage stamps.

Nellie *(filling in form)*: Thank you for your time, Mr. Black. I hope to have the opportunity of bringing this matter before the next convention of insurance men.

Mr. Black: The insurance men have invited you to speak to them?

Nellie: Not yet. But they will.

(Nellie exits downstage right. Mr. Black exits downstage left, taking the sign "Neepawa Insurance Agency" with him. He leaves the desk in area 3. Crossfade — lights come up in areas 2, 4, and 5 as they go down in area 3, and Lillian and Frances enter from upstage right.)

Scene   **The Temperance Lecture**

Lillian *(sitting, facing front in area 4)*: It looks like everyone's here. What a good crowd.

Frances *(moving downstage into area 2)*: We are proud to have with us today Miss E. Cora Hind, the Agricultural Editor of the Winnipeg Free Press. Miss Hind. *(Cora enters from upstage left, carrying an easel and a number of large white cards. To Cora)* May I help you?

(Frances takes a chair from area 1, places it in area 2 beside the

easel which Cora sets up. Cora hands Frances the white cards.)

Cora: Thank you. *(Cora faces audience in area 2. Frances sits, facing front)* Good afternoon. Have you ever seen a spider entice a silly fly into its cobweb? Have you ever watched as it drained the last drop of blood from its victim? Just so does alcohol lure its victim. Just so does the drink traffic drain the lifeblood of the nation. It is the moral sepulchre in which are buried some of the most promising beginners in life's battles. Let me quote to you from a report of a special committee of the Legislative Assembly of Canada. This survey is based on one hundred families studied over a five year period. Number of drunks in one hundred families . . . .

Frances: Two hundred and fourteen. *(She places a card which reads 214 on the easel.)*

Cora: Number of widows left . . . .

Frances: Forty-six. *(She places a card which reads 46 on the easel.)*

Cora: Number of orphans . . . .

Frances: Two hundred and thirty-five. *(She places a card which reads 235 on the easel.)*

Cora: Number of premature deaths due to drunkeness . . . .

Frances: Two hundred and three. *(She places a card which reads 203 on the easel.)*

Cora: Number of years of human life lost through drunkenness . . . .

Frances: One thousand, nine hundred and fifteen. *(She places a card which reads 1,915 on the easel.)*

Cora: These are not just idle numbers on a card. I have travelled throughout the west and I have seen the defeated men, the broken families, the abandoned farms and the battered women and children. It is the women who suffer the most. Without property rights, they cannot protect their farms. Without guardianship rights, they cannot protect their children. Let us pray that when women get the vote, which they will, they will use it as a weapon and cast their votes for prohibition. *(Frances places the card "Prohibition" on the easel)* Prohibition! It's a hard sounding word, hard as a locked door. But the drink traffic is always with us. It stalks our streets. It throws its challenge in our faces. In order that we may go forward into the glorious future that Canada holds out to us, we must accept this challenge. When science discovered the relationship between the housefly and typhoid, the mosquito and yellow fever, the breeding places of these insects were wiped out. Now, these epidemics are almost unknown. Alcohol is an epidemic. Every man, woman and child here today must ask himself, "Am I part of the world's disease, or am I part of the world's cure?" Thank you.

Frances: Thank you, Miss Hind. That was a fine speech, indeed. And now, we would like to render for you one of our most popular numbers. Page forty-nine in your songbooks. Please omit verse three.

(Lillian, Frances and Cora move downstage centre and sing. Areas 2, 4, and 5 fade to darkness — spot comes up on women, centre. The song is "Going Dry".)

Women: Hearken brave crusaders to the message cheering
Temperance waves are rising round us mountain high.
Over all the land, saloons are disappearing
Cities, towns and hamlets all are going dry.

Carman's going dry
Sperling's going dry
Pass along the watchword
Brandon's going dry.

Carman's going dry
Sperling's going dry
Pass along the watchword
Brandon's going dry.

To the front, crusaders, where the fight is waging
For the liquor traffic has been doomed to die.
Gird you on the armour and the foe engaging
Pass along the watchword, your town's going dry.

Carman's going dry
Sperling's going dry
Pass along the watchword
Brandon's going dry.

Carman's going dry
Sperling's going dry
Pass along the watchword
Brandon's going dry.

(Spot out. Lillian and Cora exit upstage right in black. Cora strikes the easel. Frances places chair in area 5 and sits as Nellie enters area 1 and sits. Roblin enters area 3 as area 3 lights come up. He is smoking a big cigar and carrying a Union Jack which he places on the desk. Fletcher follows, carrying an ashtray and some papers. He gives the papers to Roblin and Roblin begins to look them over.)

Scene Who Is This Nellie McClung?

Roblin: Who is this Nellie McClung?

Fletcher: Oh, you know, sir. She's that madwoman. "Drink Is The Devil's Brew." "Stampede For Suffrage." She writes those trashy novels, too.

Roblin: Trashy, eh? *(Smiling)* Somewhat prurient, Fletcher?

Fletcher: No, no. They're temperance tracts in disguise. I read one of them. All about an Irish family that didn't drink. Hah. "Sowing Seeds in Danny", it was called.

Roblin: "Sowing Seeds in Danny!" Adelaide reads that.

Fletcher: Poison her mind.

Roblin: What does she want to see me for?

Fletcher: Mrs. McClung, sir?

Roblin: What the deuce, Fletcher. She phoned me up. Wants me to see some damned fool factory or other. I mean, Fletcher, that's not my job.

Fletcher: Quite right, sir.

Roblin: And what's all this about a female factory inspector? What do they want a woman in there for?

Fletcher: I dunno, sir. I'll take care of it. No need to bother yourself with such a small matter. *(Pause)* Course, if you don't go, they'll undoubtedly persuade Norris to. He's such an opportunist. *(Pause.)*

Roblin: You know, Fletcher. I think the fresh air will probably do me good. Besides, I'd like to meet this McClung woman.

(Blackout. Roblin remains seated onstage and Fletcher exits downstage left. Fletcher strikes the Union Jack and papers. Nellie enters upstage left. Frances enters upstage right. Lights full up suddenly in areas 2, 4, and 5. Nellie is standing, chair in hand and talking across the stage to Frances, who is also standing, chair in hand.)

Scene **The Ride To The Factory**

Nellie: What a lovely car.

Frances: So roomy.

(Roblin, chair in hand, walks into area 2, from area 3. During Roblin's next speech, Frances and Nellie place their chairs side by side diagonally, facing downstage left — Nellie's chair slightly upstage of Frances' chair. Roblin places his chair a few feet in front of the two behind, slightly to the left of Nellie's to suggest a car. Music plays "Rondino" softly under the following scene.)

Roblin: This, madam, is a Pierce Arrow. I had it made to my own specifications. *(He opens door and Frances and Nellie get into car. Frances sits stage right and Nellie sits stage left)* Twelve cylinders. Very powerful. *(Roblin pokes his head through the window)* You'd be wise to hold on to the straps. *(He dashes to the front of the car and cranks it up. Shouting)* Teak dashboard, hand tooled leather. It's one of the rewards of hard work.

Nellie *(to Frances)*: I've never seen cut glass vases in a car before.

Frances *(leaning out of window and shouting to Roblin)*: I love the smell of carnations.

(The car starts. Roblin gets into the driver's seat. Nellie and Frances jiggle as the car idles.)

Roblin: I have them picked fresh every day. *(He releases the hand brake and puts car into gear)* They were my mother's favourite. *(The car lurches forward, pitching the women forward with it)* Sorry.

Nellie *(jolted)*: Not at all.

Roblin: Yes, I believe in hard work. My mother worked from dawn to dusk and never seemed to complain. *(He beeps the klaxon — horn sound offstage)* Damned dogs. *(Nellie looks out window at disappearing dog)* Even used to make her own soap. Now you can buy it at the corner store. You modern young women have all these new-fangled gadgets — electricity, wringer washers, Hoovers. *(He makes a left turn, leaning into the turn. The women follow Roblin's lead, and lean to the left)* Hard day's work never hurt anyone. As a boy, I was up at sunrise and before. Happiest days of my life, running barefoot through the apple trees. *(The car leaps over a bump in the road, jostling the women)* Sorry.

Nellie: Not at all.

Roblin: Women's hearts are often too kind. Perhaps you're a little oversentimental about factory conditions. Most of these young factory girls just want to get out of the house and earn a little pin money.

Nellie: They certainly don't make enough to live on.

Roblin: Well, most of them are foreigners anyway. They were used to hard work over there, and don't expect to be lifted to the skies on a flowery bed of ease. *(Turns to talk over his shoulder)* Madam, extravagant women are the curse of the age.

(Frances sees the factory approaching rapidly.)

Frances *(alarmed)*: Here we are, sir. *(Roblin slams his foot on the brakes and honks the klaxon frantically — horn sound from offstage. Violin sounds a long note)* Oh, oh, oh, oh.

(Frances and Nellie brace themselves. The car stops and Roblin and Frances are thrown forward and back against the seats. Nellie falls off the seat. Roblin looks back and cannot see Nellie.)

Roblin: Mrs. McClung? *(Frances helps Nellie up)* Mrs. McClung! *(Roblin opens door, gets out of driver's seat and rushes to open door beside Nellie. He helps her out of the car)* Sorry.

Nellie: Not at all.

(Roblin, Nellie and Frances destroy the illusion of the car by placing

a chair each upstage centre, facing front and side by side, as Mr. Ackroyd enters from downstage left, carrying a kerosene lantern. He places the lantern on the desk in area 3 and continues into area 2.)

Scene The Factory

Mr. Ackroyd: Mr. Premier.

Nellie: Good morning, Mr. Ackroyd.

Mr. Ackroyd *(ignoring Nellie)*: Good day, Mr. Premier. So good to see you. We are honoured to have you visit Ackroyd, Acme and Associates.

Roblin: My pleasure.

Mr. Ackroyd *(takes oratorical stance)*: I am pleased and happy, and I'm sure that the late Mr. Acme would also be pleased and happy, to welcome you to our factory. I would like to present you with this miniature tractor as a momento of this auspicious occasion.

(Frances and Nellie applaud.)

Roblin: Thank you, Mr. Ackroyd. Ladies. I am sure that my grandson will while away many happy hours with this, plowing through Mrs. Roblin's gladiolas. *(Mr. Ackroyd, Nellie and Frances laugh politely. Pause)* Shall we begin, Mr. Ackroyd?

Mr. Ackroyd: Certainly. But before we move off, one word of caution. There is a lot of noise and we shall have to stick together for safety's sake.

Roblin *(gallantly)*: The ladies shall be my special charge.

Mr. Ackroyd: This way.

(Ackroyd, followed by Frances, Nellie and Roblin, moves downstage left into area 3. Crossfade from areas 2, 4, and 5 to area 3. Ackroyd lights lantern.)

Frances: All the modern conveniences, eh, Mr. Ackroyd?

Mr. Ackroyd *(the irony is lost on him)*: Yes.

(Mr. Ackroyd, followed by Roblin, Nellie and Frances, moves around desk to stage left. Area 3 starts to fade. They move upstage as if along a narrow passageway and the lantern provides the only light. The factory workers enter area 2 in black and begin to create an industrial machine. They do this using rods, chains, blocks, etc. — any material or object which suggests violent sound and motion. In this scene, the advantage of using extra players is obvious.)

Frances: My, it certainly is dark in here.

Nellie: And damp.

Mr. Ackroyd: Renovations.

Frances: Temporary inconvenience.

(When Mr. Ackroyd, Roblin, Nellie and Frances are in line with the three upstage chairs, the factory specials come up, backlighting areas 2, 4, and 5. Mr. Ackroyd climbs up on the first chair and walks across the chairs, crouched down, as if he were in a low tunnel. The other three follow. Mr. Ackroyd steps off the third chair into area 4. He ducks his head. Roblin steps off, and mimes bumping his head.)

Mr. Ackroyd: Watch your head.

(The noise of the factory is deafening and everyone shouts. Roblin slips on the floor.)

Roblin: Doesn't anyone ever sweep this floor?

(Mr. Ackroyd doesn't hear the question and smiles.)

Nellie: They don't have time. They're on piece work.

Roblin: Pardon?

Nellie: They're on piece work.

Roblin: What?

Frances: They're paid by the piece.

(Roblin strains to hear and does not watch where he is going. The nature of the machine will determine the next action but Roblin is

either caught in the machine or hit by it. He narrowly misses a serious accident.)

Roblin *(shouting desperately)*: Ackroyd, Ackroyd, Ackroyd!

(Ackroyd, Nellie and Frances stop moving.)

Mr. Ackroyd: Stop the machine!

(The machine stops. There is great noise and confusion and everyone speaks at once.)

Mr. Ackroyd: Are you alright, sir?

Roblin: Yes.

Mr. Ackroyd *(to workers)*: You'll be fired for this. This is all your fault, you clumsy idiots.

Girl 1: You can't do that. It was her fault.

Girl 2: It wasn't my fault. It was his fault. Why didn't he look where he was going? Tell me that.

Girl 1: Tell me that. Why didn't he look where he was going?

Frances: Are you alright, Sir Rodmond?

Roblin: Yes, thank you.

Nellie: Are you alright?

Roblin: Yes, yes, yes! *(Mr. Ackroyd starts to exit upstage right. Roblin shouts above the noise)* Ackroyd!

Mr. Ackroyd: Yes, sir?

Roblin: I want these factories cleaned up.

Mr. Ackroyd: Right away, sir.

(Mr. Ackroyd exits upstage right. Roblin moves into area 3, followed by Nellie and Frances. Area 3 comes up.)

Roblin: Why do you women bother yourselves with these things?

Nellie: Somebody has to.

Frances: Your factory inspectors don't do their jobs. Perhaps a woman would be more conscientious.

Roblin: What the deuce, madam. What on earth could a woman do?

Nellie: She could begin by taking the Premier on a factory inspection tour.

Frances *(consulting her notebook)*: Ferguson and Sons. 10:15 a.m.

Roblin: Thank you, ladies. I've seen enough. I'll admit I'm shocked and I'll speak to Fletcher first thing in the morning.

(Roblin, Nellie and Frances exit downstage left. Ackroyd enters upstage left and throws a broom at the factory workers.)

Mr. Ackroyd: Sweep up this floor.

(Ackroyd exits downstage right. The workers move into area 2, desultorily sweeping.)

Girl 1 *(bursting into tears)*: I can't lose this job. I can't.

Girl 2 *(stopping sweeping)*: But, why?

Girl 1 *(wailing)*: Listen. *(Music: Intro to "Father's A Drunkard, And Mother Is Dead". The factory specials go out and a spot focuses on workers. Girl 1 sings the verses. Girl 2 joins in on the chorus)*
>We were all so happy till Father drank rum
>Then all our sorrow and trouble begun;
>Mother grew paler and wept every day,
>Baby and I were too hungry to play.
>Slowly they faded, and one summer's night
>Found their dear faces all silent and white;
>Then with big tears slowly dropping, I said:
>Father's a drunkard, and Mother is dead!
>
>Mother, oh! Why did you leave me alone,
>With no one to love me, no friends and no home?

Dark is the night, and the storm rages wild,
God pity Bessie, the drunkard's lone child!

Oh! If the "Temp'rance men" only could find
Poor, wretched Father, and talk very kind.
If they could stop him from drinking, why, then
I should be so very happy again!
Is it too late? "Men of Temp'rance" please try.
Or poor little Bessie may soon starve and die.
All the day long I've been begging for bread—
Father's a drunkard, and Mother is dead!

Mother, oh! Why did you leave me alone,
With no one to love me, no friends and no home?
Dark is the night, and the storm rages wild,
God pity Bessie, the drunkard's lone child!

(Spot out. Factory workers exit upstage right, striking whatever material has been used for industrial machine. Nellie enters from upstage left and walks into area 2. Area 2 — lights up.)

Scene   **The Convention of Insurance Men**

Nellie: I would like to thank the Registered Insurance Agents of Manitoba for inviting me to speak to them today. I would like to say a few words about the Elections Act. A lunatic may regain his reason and be given his vote back. A criminal may vote again after he's let out of prison, and isn't it strange how the government manages to let him out just before an election? *(Applause from offstage)* On the other hand, if a man becomes an idiot, his vote is taken away. *(Applause from offstage)* A woman can't lose what she's never had. Thank God for small mercies. *(Applause from offstage.)*

(Blackout. Nellie exits downstage left. Roblin enters area 4. Lights come up in area 4. Roblin is wearing a carnation in his buttonhole.)

Scene   **Breakfast With Adelaide**

Roblin: Adelaide, have you seen my homburg?

(Adelaide enters from downstage right, carrying a homburg and two books. She is wearing a frilly breakfast cap.)

Adelaide: I have it right here, dear. I was just giving it a brush.

Roblin: Thank you. *(He puts hat on at a jaunty angle and straightens his tie.)*

Adelaide: You look very spruce, Roddy.

Roblin: Thank you.

Adelaide: You're certainly in a hurry. You didn't even eat your egg.

Roblin: Pressing affairs of state, my dear. *(He whistles a few bars of "The Maple Leaf Forever" and fixes carnation in buttonhole.)*

Adelaide: They say that Mrs. McClung is a most attractive woman.

Roblin *(noncommital)*: Indeed?

Adelaide: And terribly charming.

Roblin: We'll see. *(Adelaide holds out the two books, "Sowing Seeds in Danny", for Roblin)* Adelaide. No!

Adelaide: Oh, please, dear. Just two tiny autographs. I promised Hettie Ferguson one, and one for myself. I'm sure Mrs. McClung won't mind.

Roblin: I mind, Adelaide.

Adelaide: Hettie will be so angry if I don't get her one. Please, Roddy, please.

Roblin *(takes books)*: Suffering peanuts.

(Crossfade area 4 to area 3. Roblin crosses downstage into area 3. Music: "The Maple Leaf Forever". Fletcher pushes a tea tray into area 3 on which there are two teacups and saucers, a milk pitcher, sugar bowl and sugar tongs, a plate with slices of lemon, and the Union Jack. He puts the Union Jack on the desk.)

Scene   **The Second Meeting With Roblin**

Roblin: You may show in Mrs. McClung, Fletcher. *(Fletcher hesitates)* Something troubling you, Fletcher?

Fletcher: If you don't mind my saying so sir, she has no business in the building.

Roblin: For God's sake, Fletcher. Where's your sense of chivalry? It's just this once.

Fletcher *(quietly)*: If you let one in, you let them all in.

Roblin: What's that?

Fletcher: Nothing, Mr. Premier. This way, Mrs. McClung.

(Nellie enters from downstage right. She shakes hands with Roblin.)

Nellie: Sir Rodmond, I've come here today to speak to the cabinet.

Roblin *(taken aback)*: The cabinet.

Nellie: Yes.

Roblin: What a charming idea. *(Laughs)* Will you take tea?

Nellie: Yes, thank you.

(Fletcher places chair behind Nellie and she sits stage right of Roblin. Fletcher then begins to pour the tea. Roblin taps the books.)

Roblin *(takes pen from desk drawer)*: I wonder if you'd . . . uh . . . mind . . . uh . . . .

Nellie *(takes pen and books and signs)*: Not at all.

(Fletcher holds up the milk pitcher and looks inquiringly at Roblin. Nellie looks up.)

Roblin: Lemon or milk?

Nellie: Milk, please. *(Roblin nods to Fletcher who pours the milk into the cup. Roblin smiles at Nellie encouragingly)* You see, I don't think the cabinet realizes how unfair the laws are to women.

(Fletcher lifts sugar tongs and pauses, catches Roblin's eye.)

Roblin: Sugar?

Nellie: Yes, thank you. *(Leaning in)* It occurred to me that if I could make it aware of the injustices, it would want to rectify the situation.

(Fletcher whispers in Roblin's ear.)

Roblin: One lump or two?

Nellie: Two.

(Pause. Fletcher proceeds to pour tea, then hands Nellie and Roblin the tea and they sip.)

Roblin: And how long do you think this interview will take, Mrs. McClung?

Nellie *(smiles)*: Oh, I wouldn't want to take up too much of their time.

Roblin: What makes you think that the cabinet will listen to you?

Nellie: I'm not that hard to listen to. Might brighten up their day.

Roblin *(unamused)*: Thank you, Fletcher. That will be all. *(Fletcher exits downstage left, after giving Nellie a malevolent look. Roblin is determined to be charming)* Mrs. McClung, I believe in leaving well enough alone. All these new-fangled ideas only lead to dissension and argument.

Nellie: But . . . .

Roblin: You take the Indians, for example. Before the white man came along, they were happy eating muskrat and the bark of trees. Now they've lost their good old-fashioned ways.

Nellie: Yes, but . . . .

Roblin: Now, you forget all this nonsense about women voting. Take it from me. *(Intimately)* Nice women don't want the vote.

Nellie: But they do, Mr. Premier, and I think I could make the cabinet understand why.

Roblin *(forcefully)*: Just a minute, Mrs. McClung. Enough's enough. I have no intention of allowing you to speak to the cabinet. *(Stands)*

If you'll excuse me. It's been pleasant but I have a lot of work to do.

Nellie *(intensely)*: If you don't listen to me now, you'll be sending away the best advisor you ever had.

Roblin *(heatedly)*: What if I told you I didn't need your advice. *(Regains composure)* Mrs. McClung, you've had a little bit of success at country schoolhouse entertainments, and the applause has gone to your head. *(Nellie stands)* Madam, the rights of women is a very minor issue.

Nellie: Sir Rodmond, by the time the next election rolls around, the rights of women will be a very major issue.

Roblin *(smiles)*: Is that a threat?

Nellie *(serious)*: No. It's a prophecy.

(Roblin and Nellie shake hands. Lights fade on area 3 to black. Music: Last bar of "Victory Bells". Roblin and Nellie exit downstage left.)

Act two   *In area 1, the two small desks are pushed together and surrounded by four chairs. Area 3 contains the large desk with a chair upstage right of it and one downstage left. The phone rings in black. It rings again as lights come up in area 1, and Frances enters from upstage right.*

Scene   Lillian's Idea

Frances *(picks up phone)*: Hello, Political Equality League. Yes, we do have suffrage petitions. No, they're free of charge. Alright. Thank you for calling.

(Frances hangs up phone and sits down at typewriter. She puts paper in machine and begins to type briskly. She is tired. Lillian enters downstage right.)

Lillian: Frances, dear. How good to see you.

Frances: Hello, Lillian. *(Stops typing)* How was Vancouver?

Lillian *(excitedly)*: It was just wonderful. We went walking in Stanley Park every day. We played tennis. I even went skiing. I hope you weren't too rushed off your feet.

Frances: It's been . . . .

Lillian: The University Women's Club gave me the royal treatment. They're very impressed with the work we are doing. How are the plans for the delegation to Premier Roblin coming along?

Frances: Fairly well. I . . . .

Lillian: Oh. I forgot to tell you. I saw the most marvellous play. It was called "A Mock Parliament", and in it all the women had the vote and the men had to beg for it. *(Laughing)* Can you imagine? I really enjoyed it.

Frances: I'm glad you had a nice time, Lillian, but I hope you realize that January 27th is exactly two weeks away.

Lillian: We've got to get busy.

Frances *(exasperated)*: I have been busy. I've been writing and organizing and knocking on doors. Nellie's in Brandon, you were in Vancouver and Cora's been off, heaven knows, in a field of wheat somewhere.

Lillian *(sits)*: Oh, I am sorry. We have left you to it.

Frances: Now I've got one hundred and twenty-five delegates ready to troop into the Legislative Assembly just to hear Sir Rodmond say no.

Lillian: Frances, you're overtired. What you need is a good strong cup of tea and some cinnamon toast to perk you up.

Frances: What we need is a lot more money and a few more ideas. Sometimes, I wonder about our sanity. We've been going through all this for years, and every time we know we're going to be turned down flat.

(Lillian sighs. Frances resumes typing. Pause. Lillian laughs suddenly.)

Lillian: Isn't that marvellous!

Frances *(stops typing)*: What?

Lillian: We know we're going to be turned down flat.

Frances: What are you talking about?

Lillian: We could put on our own Women's Parliament right after the delegation — right after Sir Rodmond turns us down. What an opportunity for satire! Think of the publicity. And the money we'll make. It'll be a gala night at the Walker Theatre. I hope the theatre's not all booked up.

(Crossfade from area 1 to areas 2, 4, and 5. Cora enters from upstage right, carrying ice skates. C. P. Walker enters from downstage left, smoking a cigar.)

Scene   Booking The Theatre

Cora: Mr. Walker, Mr. Walker. Just the man I wanted to see.

Walker: Hello, Miss Hind. Skating?

Cora: I'm off to the rink. Care to join me?

Walker: No, thank you. I'm on my way to the theatre.

(They begin strolling along together.)

Cora: Mr. Walker, we had such a good time at "Ben Hur" last year. The chariot race was so exciting. Aunt Alice and I were clutching each other in delight.

Walker: Well, if you enjoyed last year's season, wait 'til you see what I've got lined up this year. Do you know I've booked George Arliss in "Disraeli"!

Cora *(stops)*:
> "For he must blaze a nation's ways
> With hatchet and with brand
> 'Til on his last won wilderness,
> An Empire's bulwarks stand."

Walker: Hmmm. Kipling.

Cora: Yes.

(They begin to walk.)

Walker: And do you know who else I've got booked? Mrs. Schumann-Heink.

Cora *(stops)*: What a great voice. I'll never forget her, standing on your stage, singing "Tristan and Isolde". I imagined her in a great field of wheat, lifting her voice up to heaven. She and Mrs. Walker are great friends, aren't they?

Walker: Yes. She's such a jolly woman. What a sense of humour she has. There's a story that when she played Washington, or Vashington as she calls it, she said, "I love to play Vinnipeg the best because my friend, Mrs. Valker, always brings me the beer". *(Walker has forgotten that Cora is a member of the W.C.T.U. Pause)* Lovely woman.

Cora: Lovely voice. *(Stops)* Mr. Walker, is the theatre booked for January the 28th?

Walker: No, I don't think so, Cora. Why?

Cora: Well, I'm here on behalf of the Political Equality League, and we want to put on a wonderful political burlesque.

(They resume walking.)

Walker: A burlesque? But Cora, you don't sing. You don't dance.

Cora: Mr. Walker, it's not that kind of a play.

Walker: Oh, I see. What kind of a play is it, then? Who wrote it?

Cora: Why, we did. We all did.

Walker *(stops)*: A Canadian play?

(Blackout. Cora and Walker exit downstage left. Music: "The Maple Leaf Forever" throughout the following scene change. Lights slowly up in all areas. Frances enters from upstage left, crosses to area 1 and strikes small desk with typewriter downstage right. Lillian enters from upstage right, wheels second desk from area 1 into area 5, upstage right of large desk in area 3. Nellie enters from downstage left, crosses

to area 1. Nellie and Frances take the four chairs in area 1 and arrange them diagonally from right to left, side by side in areas 1 and 4. Lillian takes chair upstage right of large desk and places it behind small desk. She places chair downstage left behind large desk. Cora enters from upstage left with "Vote With Women" banners which she distributes. The women put them on and stand in front of stage right chairs, Nellie in front of upstage chairs, next Cora, Lillian and Frances, respectively. Roblin, carrying Union Jack, enters from downstage left, followed by Fletcher carrying balloons. The men cross upstage centre, then left. Fletcher stands behind the small desk, still carrying balloons. Roblin crosses to large desk and sits. Fletcher and the women sit.)

Scene   **The Delegation**

Roblin *(sotto voce)*: Are the boys all here, Fletcher?

Fletcher: Yes, Mr. Premier.

Roblin *(stands)*: Members of the Committee. We are pleased to have with us today the charming members of the Political Equality League, who are here to petition for suffrage. The first spokesman — uh — spokeswoman will be Mrs. Nellie McClung. Mrs. McClung.

Fletcher: Here, here.

Nellie *(stands)*: I want to thank you for your gracious reception of our delegation. *(Applause from the women. Roblin nods graciously)* We are not here to ask for mercy but for justice. Do we not have brains to think, hands to work, hearts to feel and lives to live? Do we not bear our part in citizenship? Do we not help to build the empire? We want the women's point of view represented in our legislation. How would you, Sir Rodmond, like to be governed by a parliament of women?

Roblin: I have a good wife. She governs me well enough.

(Fletcher laughs.)

Nellie: The Premier has a good wife. He, at least, is not afraid to trust the women with the franchise. *(The women laugh)* However, there are some who say that the government is afraid to give us the vote.

Women: Here, here. True, true. Go on.

Roblin: Some people will say anything.

Nellie: Indeed, they will. Some even say that politics is too corrupt for women. But why should politics be corrupt? There is nothing inherently vicious about politics, and the politician who says it is corrupt is admitting one of two things — either that he is a party to that corruption, or that he is unable to prevent it.

(The women applaud.)

Women: Here, here. True, true. Go on.

Nellie: In either case, he is sounding the alarm and we are willing, even anxious to come to the rescue.

(The women laugh and applaud. Roblin rises in anger and interjects.)

Roblin *(shouting)*: When you say things are corrupt, it is only the imaginings of a vile and wicked mind.

(Fletcher pounds his desk.)

Women: No, no. Shame, shame. Go on, Nellie, go on.

Roblin: I did not dispute you when you were speaking. You will be good enough to listen to my reply. *(Nellie sits down. Roblin regains composure)* Now. The question raised today is not a new one, and it is not confined to Manitoba, for the claim of women for equal suffrage is being made in a great many civilized countries, mostly English-speaking ones.

Fletcher: Here, here.

Roblin: As you know, we draw our inspiration in legislation, theology, art and sicence from the motherland. Now, that being a fact that none will deny, can you, can anyone, say with confidence that what we have today will be preserved and not destroyed? So surely as the sun arose today in the east and will set in the west, so surely, if you are right, the franchise will come. But, consider the example of England. There, when Mrs. Pankhurst and her militant supporters were briefly disappointed in their cause, they became hysterical, endangered life, and destroyed millions of dollars worth of property. As I have listened, I have thought how delighted Lloyd George, Asquith, and other British statesmen would have been if they had been approached in the same ladylike manner as I have been today. A mother has a hundredfold more influence in shaping public opinion around her dinner table than she would have in the market place, hurling her eloquent phrases to the multitude. I believe that woman suffrage would break up the home. It would throw the children into the arms of the servant girls! *(The women stand, applauding vigorously. Fletcher applauds and then, hearing the applause, stops, perplexedly. Roblin turns and stares at the women. He turns to Fletcher)* Come on, boys.

(Music: "The Maple Leaf Forever". Lights slowly fade. Roblin and Fletcher, with balloons, exit downstage right, followed by Nellie, Cora, Lillian and Frances respectively. Nellie carries with her the Union Jack. Violinist begins to tune in black. Lights come up slowly in all areas.)

Scene **The Walker Theatre**

Nellie *(entering from upstage right, carrying bunting)*: I've got the bunting.

(Nellie crosses to large desk in area 3. Frances enters from downstage right, carrying newspaper. She crosses to area 3, and gives newspaper to Nellie. Nellie and Frances move large desk upstage centre. Lillian enters from downstage right.)

Lillian: I want to talk to Mr. Walker. Won't be a moment.

(Lillian crosses to small desk in area 5, wheels it out upstage left. Nellie puts newspaper on chair upstage right, and drapes bunting on large desk. Frances, facing front, talks out.)

Frances: Frank? May I please see the spotlight for the last speech?

(Blackout. Spot up, which wavers about. Cora enters from upstage right and is hit by the spot. She is carrying the balloons.)

Cora: What is going on? I can't see a blasted thing. And where is Lillian?

(The spot continues to wander about the stage. Lillian enters from upstage left with mace. Cora places balloons on stage right chairs, except for first chair, downstage right.)

Lillian: I can't find Mr. Walker. We've only got five minutes.

(She crosses upstage centre and places mace on large desk. Lillian exits downstage right.)

Frances: Oh, Frank. That will never do.

(Blackout.)

Lillian *(offstage right)*: Frances, your hat is here. Come and put it on.

Frances: Coming, Lillian. For heaven's sake, Frank. Turn something on.

(Frances exits downstage left. All areas come up. Lillian enters from downstage right, carrying hat.)

Lillian: Where's Frances?

Nellie: Trying on her hat.

(Lillian puts the hat on the large desk. Frances enters from downstage left.)

Frances: Wonderful news. We're all sold out.

All *(simultaneously)*: Marvellous. Isn't that splendid!   Hurray!

(Blackout. Nellie moves downstage centre into area 2. Cora stands in front of chair, downstage right. Lillian stands in front of chair, downstage left. Frances crosses upstage centre, puts on hat and picks up mace.)

Cora *(whispers)*: Good luck, everybody.

(Spot up on Nellie. All areas come up slowly.)

Nellie: Ladies and gentlemen, may I remind you that for the next short while, positions in society will be reversed. The women will have the vote and the men will have to beg for it.

(Spot out. All areas are up. Nellie crosses to upstage left chair and stands in front of it.)

Frances *(Speaker of the House)*: No idiot, lunatic, criminal or man shall vote. *(Raps mace three times)* I hereby declare this parliament in session.

(All converge centre stage and talk at once, as follows.)

Nellie: I just adore that mace. It's the prettiest thing.

Frances: Thank you. I love your hat.

Nellie: This old thing?

Lillian: Did you hear that Mrs. Armstrong had a boy?

Frances: Order, order, ladies.

Cora: A boy? She must be so disappointed.

Nellie: That makes five boys. Tsk, tsk.

Frances: Order, order, ladies.

Lillian: Five!

Cora: Have you seen that new Sears catalogue?

Nellie: Aren't the short skirts ghastly?

Frances: *(raising her voice)*: Order! *(Silence. Nellie, Cora and Lillian sit down. Frances, sweetly—)* Shall we begin, ladies? *(Pause)* The first item on the agenda is the question of the franchise for men.

Lillian *(as Government, stands)*: Madame Speaker. It's a well-known fact, and I speak as a mother, that the male child is more difficult to toilet train than the female child, and the same would undoubtedly hold true when training men in parliamentary procedures. *(Sits.)*

Cora *(as Opposition, stands)*: Red herring. Red herring.

Frances *(Speaker)*: Order. Order. I recognize the Honourable Leader of the Opposition.

Cora *(Opposition)*: Speaking as one who is rather keen on men, I submit that it is poppycock to shut out half of the world's population simply because of a minor biological difference. *(Sits.)*

Lillian *(as Government, stands)*: Madame Speaker, may I retort?

Cora *(as Opposition, stands)*: That's a nickel word.

Frances *(Speaker)*: Order. Order. Perhaps the Honourable member of the Opposition will allow the Honourable member from Brandon-Souris to reply.

Cora *(Opposition)*: Don't you mean retort?

Frances *(Speaker)*: Order!

(Cora — the Opposition — sits.)

Lillian *(Government)*: This difference. A minor one, you say? Let me appeal to your finer sensibilities, woman to woman. Would you want this room, this very room, filled with the reek of cigar smoke? Would you want to hear the clink of brandy glasses in caucus? Would you want the halls festooned with spitoons, echoing with ribald laughter? Think. Can you, in all honesty, still say a minor difference?

Cora *(Opposition)*: Balderdash. Poppycock. Emotional hogwash.

Frances *(Speaker)*: Order. Order. Time has expired. Chair recognises the . . . .

Lillian *(Government)*: And have you considered the suggestive nature of male attire — the coloured waist-coats, the embroidered suspenders, the bay rum behind the ears, the waxed ends of moustaches and the tight trousers? *(Sits.)*

Cora *(Opposition)*: Yes, yes, yes.

Frances *(Speaker, rapping mace)*: May I have order! We have reached the end of the question period.

Cora *(as Opposition, stands)*: I would like to address . . . .

Frances *(Speaker)*: I gather that the Honourable Leader of the Opposition has a supplementary question.

Cora *(Opposition)*: I address my question to the Honourable member from Brandon-Souris. I speak on behalf of the fathers of Manitoba. Should they not have legal guardianship rights over their children?

They plant the seed, should they not have a share in the harvest? *(Sits.)*

Lillian *(as Government, stands)*: Who brings the child forth in pain and travail? The mother. Who nurtures it at her breast? The mother. Who teaches it to walk, talk and sing?

All *(sing together)*: Put them all together, they spell. "Mother".

(Cora — the Opposition, and Lillian — the Government, speak together, neither listening to the other. They are face to face.)

Cora *(Opposition)*: Furthermore, I find it disgusting that you should use this important question as an opportunity for oratory.

Lillian *(Government)*: My husband doesn't want the vote. He's the power behind the throne. That's good enough for him.

(As they argue, a man enters from upstage left. He is wearing a banner which says "Votes For Men". He crosses downstage right and attempts to get past Lillian and Cora. They pay no attention to him. The Speaker attempts to restore order as he pushes through the two women and stands downstage right. He, the delegate, is a timid soul but he knows that right is on his side.)

Frances *(Speaker)*: Order! *(Silence. Cora and Lillian sit. Frances, sweetly—)* The chair recognizes the delegate from the Franchise for Fellows Society.

Delegate: Ladies and . . . ladies. I am here on behalf of the Franchise for Fellows Society to ask, nay to beg for the vote.
> We have been shut out too long and we're knocking at the door.
> We bring home the bacon, may we not cook it?
> We lie in the beds, may we not make them?
> We have one less rib, why not one more privilege?
> We have the brains, why not the vote?

(Pause. All look at Nellie who is hidden behind the newspaper. She slowly lowers newspaper, looks around and gets to her feet.)

Nellie *(The Premier)*: We wish to compliment the delegation on its splendid gentlemanly appearance. *(All whistle a wolf whistle)* If, with-

out exercising the vote, such splendid specimens of manhood can exist, such a system of affairs should not be interfered with. If the leader of the delegation is as intelligent as he is attractive, we should have no problem. As I have listened, I have thought how delighted Lady Lloyd George, Queen Mary, and other British stateswomen would have been if they had been approached in as gentlemanly a manner as I have been today. As to the work of woman, woman has toiled early and woman has toiled late so that the idol of her heart might have the culture and accomplishment that we see here in this man today. So surely as the sun arose today in the east and will set in the west, so surely, if we extend the vote to men, they will take a backward step — and fall off their pedestals. Why upset yourselves? Politics is an unsettling business, and unsettled men mean unsettled bills, broken furniture, broken vows and divorce! *(The women and the delegate gasp in horror)* Come on, girls.

(Nellie exits downstage left, followed by Lillian, Frances, and Cora, who picks up balloons and carries them out. Areas 2, 3, 4, and 5 fade to black, leaving man in area 1. Music: "Meditation From Thais" Spot up on large desk in areas 4 and 5. Man dejectedly takes off "Votes For Men" banner and walks out of area 1, which fades to black. Man crosses upstage centre into spot and whips bunting off the desk. He puts the bunting over his arm, takes area 4 chair and places it at the stage right end of desk. He crosses to upstage left chair and places it at the stage left end of desk. He takes a spoon and knife out of coat pocket and lays the table. Then, he takes an eggcup from another pocket, puts it on the table, takes an egg out of another pocket and puts it in the eggcup. He waits impassively at the stage left end of table as Roblin, on the last bars of the music, enters from downstage left. Roblin crosses into spot and sits in the stage left chair. Man exits downstage left. Lights come up in areas 4 and 5. Spot out. Roblin takes napkin off table and spreads it in lap. He looks about for his paper.)

Scene   **Reading The Reviews**

Roblin *(calling)*: Adelaide, have you seen my Telegram?

(Adelaide enters from upstage right, carrying two newspapers under her arm. She is wearing her frilly breakfast cap.)

Adelaide: I have it right here, dear. I want to read the reviews. *(Sits in stage right chair and opens newspaper)* Oh, I do wish I'd been there. *(Scanning paper)* I can never find anything in this . . .

oh, here it is. It says here: "From the standpoint of entertainment, it was excellent and few burlesques have ever met with a heartier response than last night's satire on the system of the government as it exists today." *(She hands the newspaper to Roblin which he straightens out and begins to read. Adelaide opens the other paper)* Hettie Ferguson went and she bought a new hat for it — blue with maribou . . . . I wonder what Frances Beynon has to say in the Grain Grower's Guide? "That in presenting this entertainment the Political Equality League has covered itself in glory is generally admitted throughout the city." *(Roblin puts down his paper, preparatory to eating his egg, and picks up his knife)* Oh. This would be of interest to you, dear. "Mrs. Nellie McClung, as Premier . . . as Premier," *(laughs)* . . . isn't that delightful . . . *(Roblin picks up his paper again)* "gave a hard, relentless and absolutely final negative. The arguments were so delightfully reminiscent of the speech addressed to the women recently by *(she looks up — Roblin lowers newspaper slightly)* one high in authority *(her voice trails off)* that the audience was convulsed in laughter." *(Adelaide pats Roblin's hand)* Oh. Oh. Never mind, dear. *(Roblin coughs softly from behind newspaper. Pause. Absentmindedly—)* Still, this might make all the difference. We might get the vote after all.

Roblin *(looking over paper)*: What do you mean, "we"?

(Adelaide rises hurriedly.)

Adelaide: I'll just get your coffee. Won't be a minute.

(Adelaide exits upstage right. Roblin watches her go. He picks up knife and cracks egg. He looks at it despondently.)

Roblin *(standing and calling)*: Adelaide. This egg is runny!

(Blackout. Fletcher enters from downstage right, carrying balloons. Roblin crosses downstage centre to area 2. Crossfade from areas 4 and 5 to area 2.)

Scene   Taking The Vote

Fletcher: Therefore, let it be resolved, that in the opinion of the House, such amendments should be made to the Manitoba Elections Act as will enable women to vote at elections for Members of the Legislative Assembly.

Roblin: Boys. I would consider the passage of this legislation a want

of confidence in this government.

Fletcher: Let the roll be called.

(Throughout the calling of the roll, Fletcher manipulates the balloons so that, in turn, each one bounces.)

Roblin: Armstrong.

Fletcher: Nay.

Roblin: Argue.

Fletcher: Nay.

Roblin: Bernier.

Fletcher: Nay.

Roblin: Caldwell.

Fletcher: Nay.

Roblin: Ferguson. *(Pause. Both Roblin and Fletcher look at one balloon)* Ferguson.

(The balloon bounces.)

Fletcher: Nay.

(Roblin speeds up the roll call. The balloons bounce in a frenetic fashion and Fletcher continues to interject, "Nay".)

Roblin: Harvey, Howden, Hughes, Lawrence, Lyons, Lyle, McFadden, McMeans, Montague, Orok, Prefontaine, Reid, Reilly, Steel, Taylor.

Fletcher: The amendment is hereby defeated, thirty-two to twelve.

(Fletcher hands the balloons to Roblin.)

Roblin: Thank you, boys.

(Roblin exits downstage left, carrying balloons. Exit music is "The Maple Leaf Forever". Fletcher turns to exit upstage. Spot on Fletcher.

He turns and strikes a pose. As he recites the following poem, a charwoman resets the stage. Fletcher attempts to ignore her. Charwoman enters from upstage right, wheeling on small desk. She crosses to area 1, leaves desk and exits downstage left. She enters from downstage left, wheeling on small desk with typewriter and telephone, pushes the two desks together and dusts them off with a feather duster. She places the stage right chairs around the desks. She crosses upstage centre and dusts Fletcher off as she passes him. He pauses, then continues. She wheels large desk into area 3, takes two stage left chairs and puts once behind large desk and one stage left of it. She picks up eggcup and silverware, then drops silverware at the end of the poem.)

Fletcher: A poem.

> She is not old, she is not young
> But a brave Irish lass is Nellie McClung
> With a tongue that would soothe the birds off the trees
> And bright sparkling eyes that show she's a tease.
> The ladies all love her, the men on her dote
> But what's riling Miss Nellie is they won't let her vote.
>
> Besides we all know, and the truth must be told
> Woman's sphere is the home, not out in the cold.
> She's too tender and fragile to mix with the gang
> Of Roblin's home guard, who sometimes use slang.
> So while we are sorry, it cannot be done
> Votes are for "Men Only" not Nellie McClung.

(The silverware crashes to the desk. Fletcher turns and glares at the charwoman.)

Fletcher: Thank you.

(Blackout. Fletcher and charwoman exit downstage left. The phone rings. Area 1 up. Cora enters from downstage right.)

Scene   **Election Preparations — The Opposition**

Cora *(picks up phone)*: E. Cora Hind speaking. Yes. *(Calling)* Frances. Telephone. *(Frances enters from downstage right and takes phone from Cora. Meaningfully—)* I think it's someone special.

Frances: Frances Beynon speaking. Oh. Hello, Frank. Oh, thank you. I'm so glad you enjoyed it. Did you really think so? Well, thank you.

Nellie was pretty good, too, didn't you think? Oh, uh huh. That would be fine. 'Bye, Frank. *(Hangs up the phone)* That was Frank.

Cora *(reading a letter)*: T. C. Norris wants Nellie to speak at a Liberal rally the night before the election.

Frances: Good. *(Looks at book on desk)* June is almost completely booked up. Binscarth on the eleventh, Russell on the thirteenth, Birtle on the fourteenth . . . .

(Lillian enters from downstage left. She is carrying a box of leaflets and a newspaper.)

Lillian: They burned Nellie in effigy last night.

Frances: Good night.

Cora: Where?

Lillian: In Brandon. An effigy with "Windy Nellie" on it was set on fire. Nobody knows who's responsible. *(Hands Cora a newspaper)* The government's issued an apology.

Cora *(reading)*: "No sane, sensible element in any party could so far forget the ordinary chivalry of manhood, to say nothing of common sense, as to burn in effigy a citizen who enjoys the respect of the entire province, irrespective of party. This incident may be attributed wholly to a hoodlum element."

Frances *(looking at leaflets)*: "Vote Sobriety, Vote Female Suffrage, Vote Liberal on July the 10th." Very nice.

Lillian *(takes box from Frances)*: We'd better get going, Cora. There are two hundred in here.

(Nellie enters from upstage right, as Cora and Lillian start to exit downstage left. They meet in area 2 which comes up.)

Nellie: Hello, everybody.

Frances: Are you alright?

Nellie *(laughs)*: It was an effigy they burned, not me.

Cora *(starts to exit, pats Nellie's shoulder)*: Rowdies and drunken louts. Take no notice.

Lillian: We're off to knock on doors. See you later.

Nellie: 'Bye.

(Nellie sits stage left of desk. Cora and Lillian exit downstage left. Area 2 out.)

Frances: How are the children?

Nellie: Full of beans. Do you know that Jack has taught Mark to say, "I'm only a suffragist's child and I've never known a mother's love"?

Frances: One of them is sure to end up on the stage.

Nellie: I wouldn't be surprised. *(Sighs)* It's not the speaking that's exhausting, it's the travelling.

Frances: Speaking of travelling, there's been a new development. You remember you were to speak in Gimli on the twentieth?

Nellie: Yes.

Frances: Well, Mr. Skinner called and it seems that somewhere our wires got crossed. Now they want you to speak on the fourth.

Nellie: Today's the third.

Frances: Yes.

(Crossfade from area 1 to areas 4 and 5. Frances exits downstage right. Nellie takes chair and moves into area 4. Fletcher enters from upstage right, takes chair from area 1 and moves into area 4. Millicent and Evelyn, carrying newspapers, enter from upstage left and pick up chairs from area 3. They move into area 5. Fletcher and Nellie place their chairs back to back, Nellie's facing stage right and slightly upstage; Fletcher's facing stage left and slightly downstage. Millicent and Evelyn place their chairs side by side, a few feet downstage of, and facing, Fletcher's. The four chairs suggest a train. All sit simultaneously, and as they do, they begin to move as if they were on a train. All speak as they move into position, during the crossfade, as follows.)

Scene   **Encounter On A Train**

Millicent: Now, Evelyn, I want the seat next to the window. You know I always get sick if I don't sit next to the window.

Evelyn: I'm so glad I bought these papers. I'll have something to read on the train.

(Fletcher hums the "Maple Leaf Forever".)

Nellie: Oh, well. I can have a nap on the train and put my feet up. That's small consolation, but it'll have to do.

(The train begins to move.)

Man *(offstage voice)*: First call to dinner. First call to dinner.

Millicent *(looking out of window)*: Just look, Evelyn, you can see for miles and miles.

Evelyn *(opening up a newspaper)*: I do like the political reports. All this election news is so exciting.

Millicent: It's not all that flat, though. Look, there's a hill.

Evelyn: That's nice, dear. How interesting. Here's another article about that McClung woman.

(Fletcher listens in.)

Millicent: Who?

Evelyn: Nellie McClung. She's speaking in Brandon tonight.

(Nellie hears her name and smiles.)

Fletcher *(raises hat)*: Pardon me, ladies. May I introduce myself. My name is P. T. Fletcher. I couldn't help overhearing you mention Nellie McClung.

Evelyn: Yes?

Millicent: You know her, sir?

Fletcher: Everybody knows Windy Nellie.

(Nellie listens.)

Evelyn: She seems to have created quite a stir. It says here the Liberals are getting on her bandwagon.

Fletcher: Tempest in a teapot, madam. Our beloved Premier is unbeatable. She thinks she's so smart. The Liberals are just using her. *(Intimately)* She's on their payroll.

Evelyn: Indeed?

Fletcher: She gets twenty-five dollars a day to do their dirty work. Norris wants to be Premier so badly he'll do anything to win the election.

Millicent: Oh, shocking.

Fletcher: She's shanty Irish, you know. Red face, big hands, big feet feet. Atrocious dresser. Horrible hats.

Evelyn: But Mr. Fletcher, there's a picture of her in here and she appears quite respectable to me.

Fletcher: Respectable? Her children run wild. She has seven or eight of them. My sister lives on her block and she often gives them clothes and feeds them. Bless her heart.

Evelyn: You paint a black picture. Surely, you exaggerate.

Fletcher: The truth is not always pleasant, madam.

Millicent: She sounds terribly wicked, Evelyn. Shall we stop over in Brandon tonight? I'd love to hear her speak.

Evelyn: What a good idea. And now, I'd like some dinner. *(Rising)* Good day, sir.

(Fletcher rises and tips his hat. Evelyn and Millicent exit upstage left. Fletcher is about to sit when he hears Nellie's voice behind him. He turns around.)

Nellie *(stands)*: Why, Mr. Fletcher. *(Shakes Fletcher's hand)* How do you do? I can't thank you enough for drumming up business for me. You must thank your sister for all her kindnesses to my children. I didn't know you had a sister. Such an angel of mercy. *(Nellie turns to exit upstage right and then turns back)* You know, I'm rather fond of this hat.

(Blackout. Fletcher and Nellie turn their chairs around and sit, facing us. Lillian and Cora enter from upstage left, turn the stage left chairs around and sit, facing upstage. Roblin enters from upstage right, crosses to centre, upstage of chairs. Lights up in areas 4 and 5.)

Scene   Election Preparations — The Government

Roblin: We are confident that we will sweep the province. *(Fletcher applauds)* I would like to thank *(slight pause)* all of you for turning out this afternoon. Let me just say this. Although we appreciate the innocent faith expressed by Mrs. McClung in the good intentions of the Liberals, we cannot share that faith. Furthermore, although we honour the woman, however innocent, who enters the arena of politics with good intentions, it is the woman who right nobly does a woman's work to whom we give all honour. *(Cora stands and exits upstage left. Roblin raises his voice)* We know that there are women who claim a share in the arduous task of government, thereby sacrificing the best traditions of civilized humanity . . . . *(Nellie stands, picks up chair, crosses to area 1, leaves chair and exits upstage right)* But, it is precisely the best women who will not sell their birthright — which may be said to be embodied in the popular proverb: "The woman who rocks the cradle rules the world."

(Lillian stands, picks up chair, crosses to area 1, leaves chair, and exits downstage right. Fletcher turns in his chair and he and Roblin watch her go. Fletcher stands, picks up chair. Roblin takes the remaining chair and walks with Fletcher into area 3. Crossfade areas 4 and 5 to area 3.)

Roblin: What you need is a drink.

Fletcher: No. Slows me down.

Roblin: Ah, the campaign trail is not what it used to be.

Fletcher: They're winning the support of more and more of the men.

Roblin: Yes, yes, I know. Why is that, Fletcher?

Fletcher *(pause)*: Do you suppose they're withholding their conjugal rights?

Roblin *(pause)*: No, I don't think so, Fletcher.

(Roblin takes two glasses and a whisky bottle out of his desk drawer. He pours himself one. Fletcher shakes his head "no".)

Fletcher *(eagerly)*: Maybe we could make a deal with this McClung creature.

Roblin *(drinks)*: No, I don't think so, Fletcher.

Fletcher *(intensely)*: Norris has promised them the vote. The Grain Growers Association has thrown its weight behind them. The United Farm Workers . . . .

Roblin: I know. The farmer needs a wife, not a business partner.

Fletcher: Well, what are we going to do?

(Pause. Roblin cannot come to grips with the new political picture. He pours himself another drink.)

Roblin: I'm going to stand on my record. Thirty-five years in the public service must mean something. I am the Premier of the Province.

Fletcher *(desperately)*: But sir, you can't hide behind the office.

Roblin *(firmly)*: Fletcher, I intend to stand on my record. *(Fletcher gives up trying to reach Roblin and pours himself a drink. Convincing himself)* Deuce it, man. I know what this country needs. I was here at the beginning when Portage was a sea of mud on the edge of the western frontier. *(Pause)* Did I ever tell you about the time I was in the cheese exporting business?

Fletcher: Yes, sir. You did.

Roblin: Oh. *(Pause)* You know, Fletcher, they used to call Manitoba the postage stamp province. It took a hell of a lot of work to extend that boundary to the sea. Now Winnipeg is the grain capital of the world. *(Drinks.)*

Fletcher *(automatically)*: That's right.

Roblin: Hundreds of outlying districts now have railways, roads, telephones.

(Roblin pours another drink for himself and Fletcher.)

Fletcher: That's true, sir.

Roblin: Damned Bell Telephone system has no imagination. Eyes always on the profit margin, never on public convenience. *(He raises his glass)* Fletcher, I give you the Manitoba Government Telephone system. *(Fletcher raises his glass. Roblin drinks)* I put the British flag on every schoolhouse in Manitoba.

Fletcher *(sardonically)*: The King.

Roblin *(reverently)*: The King. *(Now lost in the past)* I built the first agricultural college in Manitoba.

Fletcher *(drinks)*: The finest in the world.

Roblin: The finest in the world.

Fletcher: That's what I said.

Roblin: I provided a reasonable, workable, popular and satisfactory Workmen's Compensation Act.

Fletcher: Truly visionary.

(Pause.)

Roblin: Dreams, dreams . . . a man must have dreams. *(To Fletcher)* Sometimes, my boy, when the world has brought me low, I give reign to my wildest fancies. I see myself in flowing robe, galloping across the white hot sands. Fletcher, beneath this breast beats the heart of a son of the desert. *(Music: Introduction to "A Son Of The Desert Am I". Roblin looks tipsily at the musician)* Thank you, my dear. *(Follow spot up. Roblin sings, moving freely about the stage. Fletcher eventually joins in. They improvise steps together. Spot follows them and area 3 dims down)*

>A son of the desert am I,
>The iron clad hoofs of my horse spurn the sand.
>The wide spreading desert is peaceful and grand
>My good lance at rest, at my side hangs my brand.

My brave Arab comrades come at my command,
For a son of the desert am I.

None so dauntless and free on land or on sea,
For a son of the desert am I,
None so dauntless and free on land or on sea,
For a son of the desert am I.

I scoff at the sybarite's case so secure,
Luxurious life I could never endure:
'Tis freedom I love, though the world be obscure.
The desert's wild grandeur alone can allure,
For a son of the desert am I.

None so dauntless and free on land or on sea,
For a son of the desert am I,
None so dauntless and free on land or on sea,
For a son of the desert am I.

And I know that Zulica awaits in her tent,
The fairest in all the sunkiss'd Orient;
Whose form has the grace of the palm heaven-sent,
She will welcome her love when the storm cloud is spent,
For a son of the desert am I.

None so dauntless and free on land or on sea,
For a son of the desert am I,
None so dauntless and free on land or on sea,
For a son of the desert am I.

(Spot out. Roblin and Fletcher exit upstage right. Area 1 up as Lillian, Cora and Frances enter from upstage right.)

Scene   **After The Election**

Lillian: Well, we won in Souris. They've never gone Liberal before. I do hope the northern ridings go Liberal.

Frances: They always go Conservative, Lillian. You know that.

Lillian: Anything can happen in this election. We've made a gain of nine seats. That's unprecedented.

Cora: It's wonderful. We've got twenty-one seats.

Frances: And the Conservatives have twenty-five.

Lillian: That's hardly a landslide.

(Frances paces in the office.)

Cora: Valentine Winkler's in again.

Lillian *(to Frances)*: Tom Johnson . . . .

Cora *(to Frances)*: And Mr. Hudson.

(The phone rings. Frances hurriedly picks it up.)

Frances: Hello. Yes. *(Pause)* Oh. Thank you for calling.

(She slowly hangs up the phone. Pause.)

Cora: Well?

Frances: All three northern ridings went Conservative.

(Pause.)

Lillian: Three more for Sir Rodmond. *(Pause. Ironically—)* Who said, "If they beat us on the tenth, we'll be up on our feet on the eleventh"?

Cora: Who did say that?

Lillian *(smiling)*: Must have been that McClung woman.

(Crossfade to dim in area 1, up in area 3. A dishevelled Roblin is at his desk, trying to read some papers.)

Roblin *(muttering)*: Damned woman.

(Frances types . . . stops.)

Cora: Telephone scandal.

Roblin *(seems to hear a voice)*: What?

(Frances types . . . stops.)

Lillian: Elevator scandal.

Roblin: Hmmm?

(Frances types . . . stops.)

Frances: University site scandal.

Roblin *(to himself)*: No. That was the best place for the university. Costs a little more but you pay for what you get.

Frances: Do you know who got the contract for the law school? Thomas Kelly and Sons.

Cora: And at what a price.

Roblin *(stands, as if making a speech)*: Dr. Montague tells me that Thomas Kelly and Sons is one of the finest contract engineers in Manitoba. Isn't that so, Montague. *(Pause)* Montague?

Lillian: And do you know who has the contract for the new parliament buildings? Thomas Kelly and Sons.

Roblin: We are erecting a building that we hope will stand the test of time. When future generations have passed into history, Manitoba's provincial capital will remain standing, a credit to our city and our province.

Frances: The government's been charged with robbing the public purse of two million dollars; of conspiring with Thomas Kelly and Sons.

Roblin: But we all wanted it to be first class. Kelly had to change his plans. Simon told me so himself. Didn't you, Simon? *(Pause)* Simon? *(He looks for Simon who has deserted him)* Ferguson, where is Simon? *(He waits for Ferguson to answer. Ferguson has deserted him)* Fletcher, where is Ferguson? *(Pause)* Fletcher, Fletcher?

(Roblin exits upstage left, calling "Fletcher". Crossfade from area 3 to area 1. Nellie enters from downstage right, carrying newspapers.)

Nellie *(excitedly)*: The papers are all out.

All *(together)*: Give me one, Nellie. Thank you. I'll take that.

(They all read the newspapers. Pause.)

Nellie: Listen to this. Mr. P. T. Fletcher, Roblin's long-time parliamentary assistant, today denied any knowledge of the parliament buildings affair.

Lillian: The wretch.

Frances: Mr. Horwood has admitted that he has committed perjury, forgery, utterance, false pretenses, theft and falsifying public accounts. Good night.

Cora: How delicious. Kelly was overpaid by seven hundred and one thousand ninety-three dollars and fifty-nine cents. Oh, and his son's been overpaid, too.

Nellie: They got Dr. Simpson. Good. I almost hit that man over the head with my umbrella once.

Lillian: Nellie. I think they've had enough. The Conservatives are through in Manitoba.

All *(together, throwing their newspaper in the air)*: Hooray!

(Music: "Victory Bells". Area 1 out. Spot up on women as they sing.)

Women: Victory bells are ringing over the land we love,
 Jubilant voices singing praises to God above.
 Vigilant hosts are marching forward to meet the foe
 Fighting to get the ballot, we'll win, we know.

 Victory bells, victory bells, ringing all over the land,
 Victory bells, victory bells, hailing a triumph grand.
 Votes for women! Votes for women!
 Shout the battle cry.
 Votes for women! Votes for women!
 Victory draweth nigh.

(Blackout. Area 2 up. Roblin enters from upstage left, carrying the Union Jack.)

Scene **Roblin's Resignation Speech**

Roblin: Mr. Speaker, at the last session of the Legislature, certain serious statements were made, alleging overpayments in connection with the construction of the new parliament buildings. A Royal Commission was appointed to inquire into the whole matter. The authority or jurisdiction of the Commission is now challenged. This means considerable delay before that point can be determined by the courts. The government believes such delay is undesirable and contrary to public policy. That government also realized that, constitutionally, they were responsible for the acts of their officials. For these reasons, I have tendered my resignation to his Honour, the Lieutenant-Governor with the recommendation that he call upon T. C. Norris, Leader of the Opposition, to form a new government. I do not hesitate to say that my decision in this matter has been influenced to no small amount by the results of the general election of July, 1914. Upon that occasion, certain questions, which need not be considered now, led a large number of my former friends to withdraw their support. For my successor, I have nothing but the most kindly feelings and I trust that under his leadership, the province may enjoy a measure of prosperity and development as great as or greater than that which has marked the period during which I have had the honour to be Premier. "The old order changeth, yielding place to new, and God fulfills himself in many ways, lest one good custom should corrupt the world."

(Music: "The Maple Leaf Forever". Tobias Norris enters from downstage right and meets Roblin centre stage. Norris is carrying a Canadian Ensign flag. Roblin and Norris exchange flags. Roblin exits downstage right . . . . Offstage are shouts of hooray, and applause.)

Scene **The End**

Norris: Mr. Speaker, Honourable Members, Honoured Guests, thank you. The Liberal party is proud to have won the overwhelming mandate of the people *(cheers from offstage)* and I, as Premier of the province, am especially proud that, for the first time in history, the women of Manitoba will take their place in the Legislative Assembly. *(Cheers from offstage)* Today, January 27, 1916, the Elections Act of Manitoba has been amended to extend the franchise to women. *(Cheers and applause from offstage.)*

(Music: "Win Them, Win Them, One By One". The women enter on the introduction, Lillian and Frances from upstage left, Nellie and

Cora from upstage right. They take Norris by the arm and move downstage centre, singing. Spot up. Area 2 out.)

Women: Win new members, day by day
We'll help win them, here's the way
Just one way can this be done
We must win them, one by one.

So you win the one next to you
And I'll win the one next to me
In all kinds of weather, we'll all work together
To see what can be done.

(Roblin enters from upstage left and joins in.)

If you win the one next to you
And I win the one next to me
In no time at all, we'll have them all
So win them, win them, one by one.

(Spot focuses in on Nellie.)

Nellie: Never retract, never explain. Get the thing done and let them howl.

(Blackout.)

The end

Photo credits
(left to right)

E1 *(Diane Grant)*
E13 *(Diane Grant, Paul Brown)*
E18 *(Elizabeth Murphy, Francine Volker)*
E28 *(Jacquie Presly, Diane Grant, Geoffrey Saville-Read)*
E35 *(Back row — Jacquie Presly, Francine Volker;*
    front row — Diane Grant, Elizabeth Murphy)
E40—E41 *(Diane Grant, Geoffrey Saville-Read)*
E46 *(Diane Grant, Paul Brown)*
E53 *(Paul Brown, Geoffrey Saville-Read)*
E56—E57 *(Francine Volker, Geoffrey Saville-Read)*
E62 *(Francine Volker)*
E69 *(Diane Grant behind newspaper, Elizabeth Murphy,*
    Francine Volker, Jacquie Presly)
E75 *(Geoffrey Saville-Read)*

Costumes

Act one

Two bowler hats

Red bow tie

Mr. Black's jacket

Two aprons - factory workers
Two scarves - factory workers

Breakfast cap - Adelaide
Homburg

Act two

Fur coat - Lillian
Man's overcoat, gloves, scarf, hat - Walker
White toque - Cora
White gloves - Cora
Ice skates - Cora

Mauve hat with feathers - Frances

Breakfast cap - Adelaide

One headscarf - Charwoman

Two pair black gloves — Millicent and Evelyn
Two black veils — Millicent and Evelyn

Props **Set**

One small desk with
mailing basket
One small desk
One typewriter
One telephone
Telephone bell and batteries
One large desk
Seven chairs
One Tiffany lamp

Act one
Basket and checkered cloth
Lucy Stone pamphlet
Petition forms
Nellie's suitcase

Birdseed bag
Legal Status Of Women pamphlet

Cornell press release
Toothpick
Miss Purity poster

Lillian's mail
Pencils and pens
Mrs. Ruth McKenna's letter
Legal Status Of Women pamphlet

Cora's reports
Galley proof

Neepawa insurance policy
Request for refund form
Nib pens

Temperance lecture cards
Temperance lecture stand

Metal ashtray
Governmental papers
Cigars
Safety matches
Union Jack on stand

Klaxon horn
Miniature tractor
Kerosene lamp
Safety matches
Broom

Two novels - Sowing Seeds In Danny

Two spoons
Two cups and saucers
Sliced lemon
Tea service - pot, sugar bowl, creamer
Tea cloth

Act two
Cigar

Four "Votes For Women" banners
Balloons (approx. 20)

Bunting
Newspaper
Mace
One "Votes For Men" banner
Balloons

One eggcup
One spoon
One knife
One napkin
One Winnipeg Telegram
One Grain Growers' Guide
Egg

Newspapers

Two shot glasses
One whisky bottle

Newspapers

Union Jack
Canadian Ensign

Song titles
WIN THEM ONE BY ONE — Nellie, Frances, Lillian, Cora
GOING DRY — Lillian, Frances, Cora
FATHER'S A DRUNKARD, AND MOTHER IS DEAD — Two factory girls (Cora and Lillian)
A SON OF THE DESERT AM I — Roblin, Fletcher
VICTORY BELLS — Nellie, Frances, Lillian, Cora
WIN THEM ONE BY ONE REPRISE — Nellie, Frances, Lillian, Cora, Norris, Roblin
(Production music available upon application to Simon & Pierre Publishing Company Limited. See Copyright on page E2.)

Summary of music credits
"WIN THEM ONE BY ONE" by C. Austin Miles, from "THE VOICE OF SONG", published by the Woman's Christian Temperance Union, Evanston, Illinois, U.S.A.

"GOING DRY", words by Elisha A. Hoffman, music by George A. Minor, from "PROHIBITION SONGS", edited by Elisha A. Hoffman, published by the Ontario Woman's Christian Temperance Union, Toronto Ontario, Canada

"RONDINO ON A THEME" by Beethoven, published by Foley Limited, a subsidiary of Carl Fischer Co. Ltd., New York, N.Y., U.S.A.

"THE MAPLE LEAF FOREVER" by Alexander Muir, from "PROHIBITION SONGS", edited by Elisha A. Hoffman, published by the Ontario Woman's Christian Temperance Union, Toronto, Ontario, Canada

"FATHER'S A DRUNKARD, AND MOTHER IS DEAD", words by "Stella" (of Washington), music by Mrs. E.A.Parkhurst

"MEDITATION FROM THAIS" by Jules Massenet, published by United Music Publishing Co. Ltd., London, England

"A SON OF THE DESERT AM I", words by John P. Wilson, music by Walter A. Phillips

"VICTORY BELLS", words by E.E.Hewitt, music by Charles H. Gabriel, from "PROHIBITION SONGS", edited by Elisha A. Hoffman, published by the Ontario Woman's Christian Temperance Union, Toronto Ontario, Canada.